MY FIRST BOOK
TAIWAN

MW00934282

ALL ABOUT TAIWAN FOR KIDS

GL BED
CHILDREN BOOKS

Copyright 2023 by Globed Children Books
All rights reserved. No part of this book may be reproduced or distributed in any form
without prior written permission from the author, with the exception of non-
commercial uses permitted by copyright law.
Limited of Liability/Disclaimer of Warranty: The publisher and author make no
representations or liabilities with respect to the accuracy and completeness of the
contents of this work and specifically disclaim all warranties including without
limitations warranties of fitness of particular purpose. No warranty may be created or
extended by sales or promotional materials. This work is sold with the understanding
that the publisher and author is not engaging in rendering medical, legal or any other
professional advice or service. Further, readers should be aware that websites listed in
this work may have changed or disappeared between when this work was written and
when it is read.

Interior and cover Design: Daniel Day
Editor: Margaret Bam

For My Sons, Daniel, David and Jude

Night market in Taiwan

Taiwan

Taiwan is a **country**.

A country is land that is controlled by a **single government**. Countries are also called **nations, states, or nation-states**.

Countries can be **different sizes**. Some countries are big and others are small.

The National Chiang Kai-shek Memorial Hall

Where Is Taiwan?

Taiwan is located in the continent of **Asia**.

A continent is **a massive area of land that is separated from others by water or other natural features**.

Taiwan is situated in the **Eastern part of Asia.**

Taipei, Taiwan

Capital

The capital city of Taiwan is Taipei.

Taipei is located in the **northern part** of the country.

New Taipei City is the largest city in Taiwan.

Jiufen, Taiwan

Counties

Taiwan is divided into two main levels of administrative divisions: Special Municipalities and Counties (including County-level Cities).

The counties of Taiwan are

Changhua County, Chiayi County, Hsinchu County, Hualien County, Kinmen County, Lienchiang County, Miaoli County, Nantou County, Penghu County, Pingtung County, Taitung County, Yilan County, and Yunlin County. The county-level cities are Chiayi City, Hsinchu City, and Keelung City.

Population

Taiwan has a population of around **23.8 million people** making it the 56th most populated country in the world.

Taiwan is the most populous state that is not a member of the United Nations, with a population of over 23 million people.

Raohe Street Night Market, Taipei, Taiwan

Size

Taiwan is **36,197 square kilometres** making it the 139th largest country in the world by area.

The island of Taiwan is surrounded by the East China Sea to the north, the Pacific Ocean to the east, the Taiwan Strait to the west, and the South China Sea to the south. The central and western parts of Taiwan are dominated by mountain ranges.

Taipei, Taiwan

Languages

The official language of Taiwan is Standard Chinese. Standard Taiwan is a modern standardized form of Mandarin Chinese.

There are also many national languages spoken in Taiwan which include **Hokkien, Hakka, Formosan, Matsu and Wuqiu.**

Here are a few phrases in Standard Chinese
- **Hello: Nǐhǎo (Nee how)**
- **Thank you: Xièxiè (Shieh-shieh)**
- **You're welcome: Bù kèqì (Boo kuh-chi)**

Taipei 101

Attractions

There are lots of interesting places to see in Taiwan.

Some beautiful places to visit in Taiwanese are

- **Taroko National Park**
- **Chiang Kai-shek Memorial Hall**
- **Taipei 101**
- **Yangmingshan National Park**
- **Shifen Waterfall**

Taipei, Taiwan

History of Taiwan

Taiwan has a long and fascinating history that dates back thousands of years. The first known inhabitants of Taiwan were Austronesian-speaking peoples who arrived on the island around 6,000 years ago.

Taiwan has been a part of various empires and dynasties, including the Chinese Han dynasty, the Tang dynasty, and the Mongol Empire.

In the late 20th century, Taiwan underwent a process of democratization and liberalization, culminating in the lifting of martial law in 1987.

Customs in Taiwan

Taiwan has many fascinating customs and traditions.

- **Taiwan is known for its beautiful festivals and celebrations. The traditional Taiwanese lantern festival is held on the 15th day of the lunar new year and features colourful lantern displays and parades. Taiwanese people also celebrate the Mid-Autumn Festival by admiring the full moon.**
- **Weddings hold a special significance in Taiwanese culture. A traditional Taiwanese wedding ceremony includes a tea ceremony and the exchange of red envelopes containing money.**

Music of Taiwan

The music of Taiwan reflects the diverse culture of Taiwanese people. Taiwan has a thriving music scene, with genres ranging from **pop to traditional Taiwanese music.**

Some notable Taiwan musicians include

- **Rainie Yang - A Taiwanese singer, actress, and television host.**
- **Jam Hisao - A Taiwanese Mando-Pop singer. Hisao received Best Male Singer at the 24th Golden Melody Awards.**

Gua Bao buns with pork

Food of Taiwan

Taiwanese cuisine is influenced by the country's geography and history, with a focus on fresh ingredients and spices.

Some popular dishes in Taiwan include

- **Xiao Long Bao - Thin flour dumplings filled with a pork meatball and also a gelatinized meat stock**
- **Gua Bao - A soft fluffy steamed bun with hearty fillings such as braised pork belly, pickled mustard greens, peanut powder and coriander.**

Shifenliao Waterfall, Taiwan

Weather in Taiwan

Taiwan has a subtropical climate characterised by mild winters and hot summers. Summers are long and hot in Taiwan, lasting from April or May to September or October.

The typhoon season in Taiwan is from June to October.

Formosan black bear

Animals of Taiwan

There are many wonderful animals in Taiwan.

Here are some animals that live in Taiwan

- **Formosan black bear**
- **Formosan rock macaque**
- **Formosan Mountain Dog**
- **Leopard cat**
- **Chinese cobra**
- **Sika deer**

Tainan Confucius Temple

Temples

There are many beautiful temples in Taiwan which is one of the reasons why so many people visit this beautiful country every year.

Here are some of Taiwan's temple

- **Penghu Tianhou Temple Magong**
- **Tainan Confucius Temple**
- **Taichung Confucius Temple**
- **Wuchang Temple**
- **Taroko Eternal Spring Shrine**

Taiwan flag on baseball

Sports in Taiwan

Sports play an integral part in Taiwanese culture. The most popular sport is Baseball.

Here are some of famous sportspeople from Taiwan

- Hsieh Su-Wei - Tennis
- Wang Jianming - Baseball
- Yani Tseng- Golf

Taiwan Flag

Famous

Many successful people hail from Taiwan.

Here are some notable Taiwanese figures

- **Hsieh Su-wei - Tennis Player**
- **Chen Shui-bian - Politician**
- **Chien-Ming Wang - Pitcher**
- **Chi-ling Lin - Actor**
- **Natalie Morales-Rhodes - Journalist**

Jiufen, Taiwan

Something Extra...

As a little something extra, we are going to share some lesser known facts about Taiwan

- **Taiwan is home to one of the tallest buildings in the world, the Taipei 101.**
- **Taiwan is known for its high-tech industry and is sometimes called the "Silicon Island."**
- **One of the most popular beverages in Taiwan is bubble tea, a sweetened tea-based beverage that is usually served cold with tapioca pearls.**

Words From the Author

We hope that you enjoyed learning about the wonderful country of Taiwan.

Taiwan is a country rich in culture and beauty, with lots of wonderful places to visit and people to meet.

We hope you continue to learn more about this wonderful nation. If you enjoyed this book, consider leaving a review!

With Love

Made in United States
Troutdale, OR
11/08/2024

24585752R00026

MW00934280

Princess Zee's Alphabet Book: The ABC Picture Story
of a Modern Black Queen as African American Royalty
Text and Illustrations Copyright © 2023 by Tom B. Free

No part of this book may be used or reproduced in any manner whatsoever without written permission
except in the case of brief quotations embodied in critical articles and reviews.

www.TomBFree.com

ISBN Kindle eBook 978-1-960735-04-1 Softcover 978-1-960735-05-8 eBook 978-1-960735-06-5
This artist used multiple digital tools to create the paintings and 3D rendered-like illustrations.
First Edition

This book is dedicated to the real Princess Z, my daughter,
a Jamaican princess in every sense of the word... at least to me.

Marvels and wonders abound in our modern world but little girls all over dream of being real-life princesses.

Princess Zee is one of those girls and her imagination takes her to a world where the royalty of fantasy lives in our time.

But what do real-life princesses need to live as a queen nowadays?

You can help Princess Zee by looking at the pictures and finding all the items that start with the same letter.

Say the name of the items out loud when you find them!

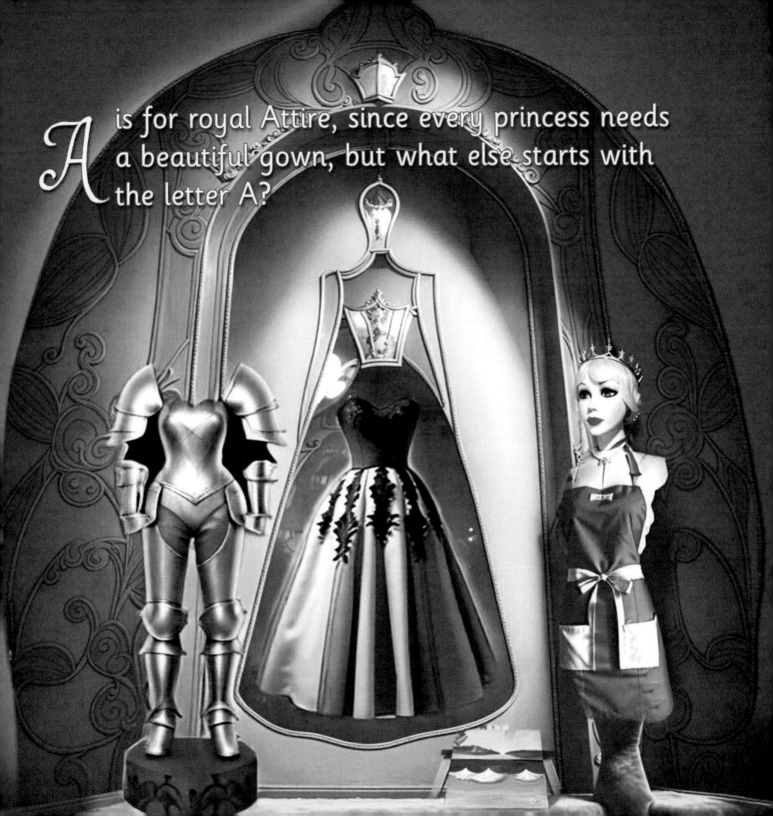

A is for royal Attire, since every princess needs a beautiful gown, but what else starts with the letter A?

B is for Bedroom, since every Sleeping Beauty needs a place to rest, but what else starts with the letter B?

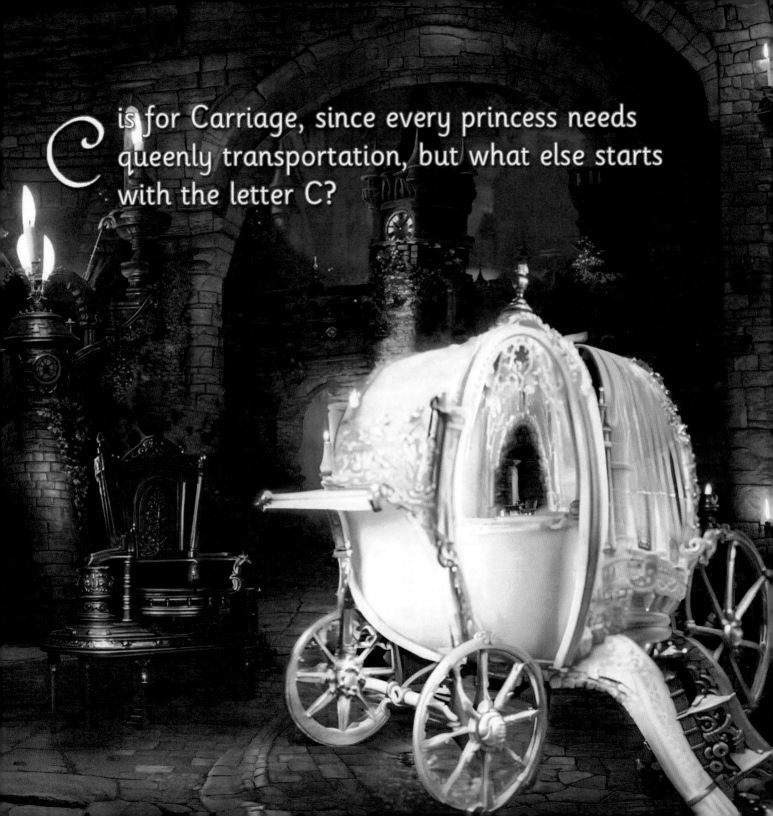

C is for Carriage, since every princess needs queenly transportation, but what else starts with the letter C?

D is for Dancing, since royalty love to go ballroom dancing, but what else starts with the letter D?

is for Easel, for artistic princesses who love to paint and draw, but what else starts with the letter E?

F is for Flowers, since every princess needs a beautiful garden, but what else starts with the letter F?

G is for Glass Slippers, since how else will her prince find his princess, but what else starts with the letter G?

H is for Hair, since every princess needs to keep up appearances, but what else starts with the letter H?

I is for Ivory Tower, since every princess needs a winter retreat, but what else starts with the letter I?

J is for Jester, since every court needs levity and laughter, but what else starts with the letter J?

K is for King, since every princess is daddy's little girl, but what else starts with the letter K?

L is for Library, since every princess needs proper learning and etiquette, but what else starts with the letter L?

M is for Magic Mirror, since every princess needs to use their imagination, but what else starts with the letter M?

N is for Noble Steed, since Princess Zee loves riding horses, but what else starts with the letter N?

O is for Outfits since Princess Zee loves dressing up, but what else starts with the letter O?

P is for Private Plane since princesses love to travel, but what else starts with the letter P?

Q is for Queen, since every princess needs a doting mother, but what else starts with the letter Q?

R is for Royal Crest, since Princess Zee's family stands for the keys to freedom, but what else starts with the letter R?

S is for Sleep since Princess Zee loves making Z's, but what else starts with the letter S?

T is for Tiara since it's the mark of royalty, but what else starts with the letter T?

U is for Unicorn since Princess Zee rides the rainbow road to outer space in her dreams, but what else starts with the letter U?

V is for Vampires since Princess Zee thinks these monsters are scary, but what else starts with the letter V?

Voila! Behold the valiant and vigilant Z, a victorious Valkyrie vanquishing a vile and venomous villain. Wearing a velvet vest, this violin-playing vampire was no match for Z's valorous strength and skill. As the vampire's fingers danced upon the strings, Z charged forward with a fearless ferocity, her sword glistening in the daylight.

But the battle was not limited to just the vampire. The vine-covered village was being sucked into a vortex, a vicious and violent violation of its inhabitants' volition. Z knew she had to act quickly, for the venal and virulent vermin responsible for this vile act were still at large.

Z embarked on her mission with a vow to vanquish these villains and guard against vice. Her valorous visitation of a bygone vexation stood vivified in her mind, fueling her with the strength to carry out her vendetta. For the only verdict was vengeance, held as a votive, not in vain. The value and veracity of such would one day vindicate the vigilant and the virtuous.

Verily, this vichyssoise of verbiage veers most verbose, but let it be known that Z's valor and virtue shone through, as she emerged victorious over the violin-playing vampire wearing a velvet vest and halted the vortex that threatened to consume the vine-covered village.

And so, with great honor, Z introduced herself to the world, holding fast to her vendetta and vowing to vanquish any and all who dared to challenge her valiant spirit.

Thankfully, Dracula only lurks in Princess Zee's nightmares fueled by late-night movies about vampies and a certain masked vigilante.

Will the Princess wake soon?

W is for Waking Up, to the great relief of a very tired Princess Zee, but what else starts with the letter W?

X is for Xeranthemum, Princess Zee's favorite flower, but what else starts with the letter X?

Y is for Yacht, Princess Zee's personal boat
the Pretty in Pink, but what else starts with
the letter Y?

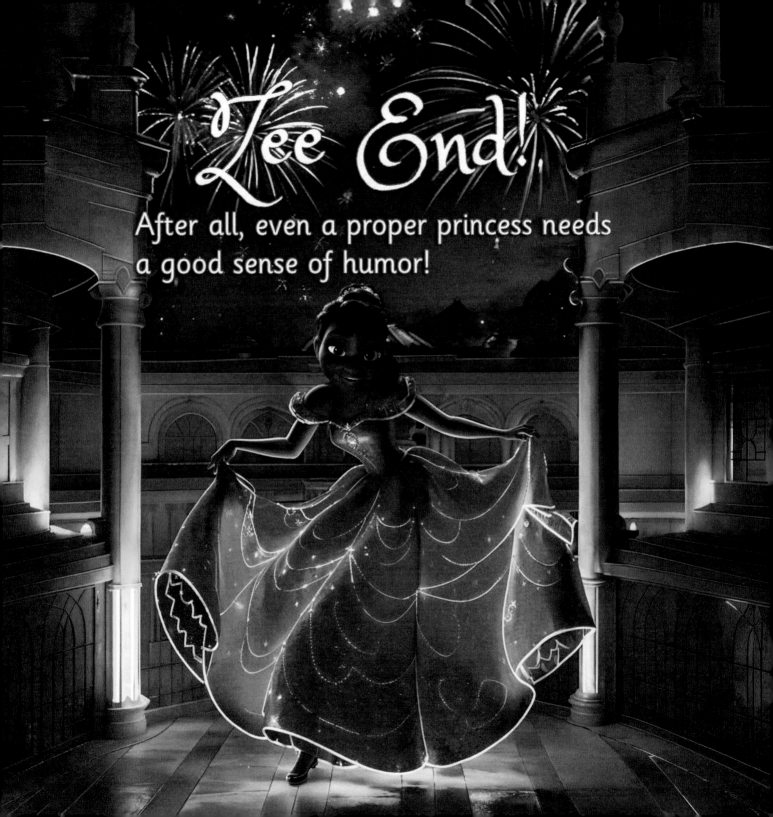

The End!

After all, even a proper princess needs a good sense of humor!

Made in the USA
Coppell, TX
19 November 2024

4054448R00021